NOTORIOUS AMERICANS AND THEIR TIMES

Boss TWEED
and Tammany Hall

by
SUZAN JOHNSON

BLACKBIRCH PRESS

THOMSON
———✦———
GALE

Detroit • New York • San Diego • San Francisco
Boston • New Haven, Conn. • Waterville, Maine
London • Munich

JB
Tweed A

Published by Blackbirch Press
10911 Technology Place
San Diego, CA 92127
Web site: http://www.gale.com/blackbirch
e-mail: customerservice@gale.com

© 2002 by Blackbirch Press,
an imprint of The Gale Group

Printed in the United States

10 9 8 7 6 5 4 3 2 1

Photo credits:
Cover, back cover, pages 50, 68, 84 © CORBIS; pages 4, 36, 57, 96, 102 © National Archives; pages 9, 30, 31, 32, 39, 44, 55, 69, 86-87, 99 © The Library of Congress; pages 12, 41, 43 © Robert N. Dennis Collection of Stereoscopic Views, Miriam and Ira D. Wallach Division of Art, Prints and Photographs, The New York Public Library, Astor, Lenox, and Tilden Foundations; pages 14, 15 © Erie Canal Museum; pages 18, 29, 90 © North Wind Picture Archives; pages 20, 51, 64, 65 © National Portrait Gallery, Smithsonian Institute; pages 21, 22, 28, 47, 54, 63, 66, 77, 78, 81, 94, 100 © Dover Publications; page 59 © King Visual Technologies; page 60 © New York Historical Society; page 74 © HarpWeek, LLC

Library of Congress Cataloging-in-Publication Data

Johnson, Suzan,
Boss Tweed and Tammany Hall / by Suzan Johnson.
        p. cm. — (Notorious Americans and Their Times)
Includes index.
Summary: Examines the life of Boss Tweed and his actions in public works, unions, fraud and graft of New York City public officials and his downfall.
        ISBN 1-56711-252-8 (hardback : alk. paper)
1. Tweed, William Marcy, 1823-1878—juvenile literature. [2. Criminals—New York, New York City—Biography—juvenile literature. 3. Organized Crime—New York, New York City—History—biography—Juvenile literature 4. United States History—1923-1978—Juvenile literature [1. Tweed, William Marcy, 1823-1878—Juvenile literature. 2. Criminals. 3. Organized crime. 4. United States—History—1923-1978 5. Unions. 2. Criminals 3. Fraud— 4. United States-History— I. Title. II. (Blackbirch Press) ·
HV6248.T17J56 2002
364.1'092-dc21   2002002475

Table of Contents

Chapter 1

*B*oss Tweed was furious. The most powerful man in the most important city in the United States had opened a weekly newsmagazine to see an image of himself in a satirical cartoon. The drawing, by a young political cartoonist named Thomas Nast, pictured Tweed as a grossly fat vulture perched over the treasury of New York City.

Tweed was not infuriated because the cartoon portrayed him as obese—he was very heavy, about 300 pounds. He was enraged by the fact that the cartoon showed—in a picture instead of words—just how powerful he had become in New York City

At the height of his power, Boss Tweed controlled the government of the city of New York.

5

government. Tweed, like many powerful political figures in other cities, controlled much of the money in the city treasury. As public works superintendent, he had approval over most public projects in New York City—as well as control over who received many of the city's 12,000 jobs. Tweed was the driving force behind the huge city's parks, paved streets, bridges, and elevated railroads. He also determined the location and the installation of sewer, water, and gas lines.

The power and influence that Tweed wielded was not unusual for a big-city public works superintendent. It was unusual, however, that every time a project was approved—every time a building went up, every time a cornerstone was laid—at least half of the public funds went directly into Tweed's pocket and the pockets of his political associates. These men belonged to the Democratic political organization known as Tammany Hall. For much of the nineteenth century in New York City, Tammany Hall controlled local politics. And, since the so-called Tweed Ring controlled Tammany Hall from 1863 to 1871, they also controlled every aspect of city government, from the mayor's office to the public works department and the thousands of workers on the city's payroll.

At the height of Tweed's power, the citywide corruption fostered by Tammany Hall had reached epic proportions. By 1870, Tweed held not one, but multiple key offices in New York City government. He simultaneously held the offices of superintendent of public works, county supervisor, state senator, Grand Sachem (leader) of the Tammany Hall Society, chairman of the Democratic-Republican General Committee of the City of New York, and supervisor of the county courthouse.

In 1871, the city's leading anti-Tammany Hall newspaper, the *New York Times*, voiced outrage in an editorial: "No Caliph, Khan, or Caesar has risen to power or opulence more rapidly than Tweed (the first). There is absolutely nothing—nothing in the city which is beyond the reach of the insatiable gang who have obtained possession of it."

As strong as those words were, they had little effect on Tweed. The *Times* was a paper of the wealthy elite who themselves were making fortunes in the booming economy. Tweed's main support came from the un-educated immigrants of New York City who had come to its shores within the previous three decades in search of a better life. As long as he kept those people in jobs that paid decent wages, Tweed believed, he had nothing to fear from the upper class—or the law.

Cartoons, however, were different from editorials and incriminating articles. The particularly scathing cartoons of Nast sent Tweed into a rage. There was no mistaking the point of these illustrations—and there was no need to add words to explain the picture. Tweed knew the cartoons could hurt him more than any number of words ever could—and they could hurt him most among the people who supported him. "I don't mind what the papers write about me," he said. "My constituents can't read. But damn it, they can see pictures!"

Nast's cartoons and subsequent incriminating coverage by the *New York Times* did a great deal to sway public opinion against Tweed and Tammany Hall. As corruption was uncovered at the highest levels of government, demand for sweeping government reforms began to take hold. By 1870, a number of powerful political forces were at work to unseat Tweed and destroy his network.

Tweed's eventual downfall came in 1871, early in an era that became known as the Gilded Age. Begun at the end of the Civil War in 1865, the Gilded Age was

"STOP THIEF!"

This Thomas Nast cartoon accuses Tweed and his cronies of pretending to be good citizens by expressing outrage at stories that the New York City treasury was being raided.

the longest period of economic growth in American history. During this period, huge advances in industrialization fueled the growth of factories, and cities sprawled both outward and upward. As skyscrapers changed the contours of city skylines, newly laid railroad tracks, train stations, and mail depots changed the contours of much of rural America.

The story of Boss Tweed and the story of the Gilded Age are intertwined. The robust growth of New York City during Tweed's time exemplified the industrial boom in urban America and laid the foundation for the growth of huge corporations that typified the Gilded Age. This incredible economic expansion, however, had its dark side as well as its obvious benefits. On the positive side, jobs were created for hundreds of thousands of Americans—many of them immigrants. More jobs and improvement of city real estate, in turn, fueled the growth of other services and manufacturing industries.

On a national level, such growth offered unique opportunities for enterprising investors to amass huge fortunes. Men such as Andrew Carnegie, Cornelius Vanderbilt, and John D. Rockefeller built financial empires by fulfilling the demand created by the development of railroads and the growth of cities. Other men, such as Tweed, exploited the excesses of these times and seized the opportunity to make their own fortunes by promoting a system of corruption and deceit. A close look at the times in which Boss Tweed thrived sheds light not only on a pivotal and unique period in American history, but also on a powerful and influential individual who did much to shape a fascinating era.

Chapter 2

NEW YORK
BORN AND BRED

*W*illiam Marcy Tweed was born on Cherry Street in Manhattan on April 3, 1823, the fourth generation of his family to reside in New York City. Over the years, the Tweeds had built a chair-making business that was well established in the city when William was born.

New York in the early 1820s was a port city with a population of more than 100,000. Many were native-born, but some had arrived in a five-year period before Tweed's birth. They were immigrants who had come to America to work on the greatest construction project of its time—the Erie Canal, which was begun in 1817. When this 363-mile waterway was completed

in 1825, it stretched across the state from Lake Erie to the Hudson River. It also made New York City the center of trade on the East Coast, with waterways that connected the metropolis to the farms and factories of the Midwest. The canal also supported immense growth in regions that were served by the waterway, because it made transportation of goods much less expensive and more accessible to many areas of the country.

As young William Tweed was growing up, New York City was fast becoming the financial center of the country. By 1830, there were more banks in Manhattan than in anywhere else in the United States. Money to finance the Erie Canal was loaned to construction companies by the biggest New York City banks. Workmen's wages, money from canal tolls, and loan repayments were all deposited in these banks. Stocks, bonds, and other investments were bought, sold, and traded by city banks as well as financial institutions from around the world.

Upon the completion of the Erie Canal, some workers headed west to seek their fortunes. Others, however, settled in New York City and sought jobs in industry or shipping. It was an exciting time, and

Canal Street, New York City, just west of Broadway, around 1820

BUILDING THE ERIE CANAL

In 1817, construction began on the Erie Canal. The canal stretched more than 360 miles from Lake Erie to the Hudson River, which empties into the Atlantic Ocean. This route created a faster and cheaper way to transport goods and people across the growing new nation.

During the eight years of construction, workers dug 363 miles of canal and built 83 locks. The locks were needed to raise and lower the

Erie Canal construction at Lockport

canal boats over the varied topography of upstate New York. Each lock could raise or lower a boat 6 to 12 feet.

In addition to digging the canal and building the locks, workers also had to construct 18 aqueducts, raised structures designed to carry water. The aqueducts on the Erie Canal were built big enough to allow the canal boats to float over places where digging and locks would not work—

low valleys, rough ground, and other bodies of water.

The work of digging the canal was arduous. People worked with shovels, picks, axes, and horses to clear a 60-foot-wide path for the canal—40 feet for the canal ditch itself, 10 feet for a work area, and 10 feet for a towpath on one side. (Although goods traveling along the canal would move by boat, the boats would be pulled by horses and mules.) Much of this labor took place in previously untouched wilderness. Trees were cut, stumps were pulled, and hills were flattened to ensure that the canal would be as level as possible.

Although the first workers on the canal were primarily farmers, they proved an unreliable source of labor because they would take time off from the construction if there was work that needed to be done at home. Canal officials solved this problem by recruiting laborers from the hordes of newly arrived immigrants who lived in the cities. The governor of New York, DeWitt Clinton, even went so far as to release people from prison if their offenses were not too serious and if they were willing to work off the rest of their sentences on the canal. Workers were paid by the day or according to how much material they removed from the work site.

Once the construction of the canal had proceeded as far as Montezuma Swamp, west of Syracuse, workers faced not only backbreaking labor but also the increased risk of illness. The oozing mud of the swamp was difficult to remove, and workers often found themselves trying to dig while standing chest-deep in water. Even worse than the water and mud, however, were the diseases that struck as many as 1,000 workers during the summer of

"Marriage of the Waters" ceremony, 1825

1819. Malaria, typhoid fever, pneumonia, and other diseases killed many workers, although the exact number is not known.

Despite its dangers, work on the canal continued, and in the fall of 1825, the project was finished. The vessel *Seneca Chief* began a journey west from Buffalo starting on October 26. When the *Seneca Chief* completed its travels along the canal, down the Hudson River, and into New York City on November 4, a special ceremony was held. Governor Clinton, traveling on the *Seneca Chief,* had brought with him vials of Erie Canal water and water from rivers around the world. The *Seneca Chief* was towed out to where the Hudson joins the Atlantic Ocean, and the containers were emptied into the ocean. This symbolically joined Lake Erie with the Atlantic Ocean and with the other great waterways of the world.

young Bill Tweed grew up while both wealth and workers flooded into his native city.

A lively and outgoing boy, Tweed lived on the Lower East Side of Manhattan and often played in the muddy streets and swam in the Hudson and East Rivers off city docks. He attended public school until eighth grade—few public-school students in New York at the time progressed beyond that level. Tweed also spent a good deal of his youth learning the family chair-making business, in addition to apprenticing as a saddler, learning the bookkeeping trade, and working in his father's brush-making company.

Throughout Tweed's teen years, ships filled with immigrants from Europe continued to arrive in New York Harbor. The city government, however, was totally unprepared for this tidal wave of newcomers. There was no organized police force and no sanitation department—except for the pigs that roamed the streets eating garbage. Most of the new immigrants teemed into the Lower East Side. Others built shacks in the swampy area of central Manhattan, where Central Park is located today. Still others claimed a place in the northern outskirts of the city—in the quiet farming village known as Harlem.

In 1844, at age 21, Bill Tweed married Mary Jane Skaden, the daughter of one of his father's business partners. As expected, Tweed went into the family's chair-making business. The young New Yorker's real love, however, was the fire department. He had joined a volunteer neighborhood unit at age 16 and spent 11 years at the local station, eventually rising to foreman.

Fires were a constant danger in the early 1800s—they destroyed much of lower Manhattan in both 1837 and 1845—and firefighting was an exciting life for a young man. Fire departments in the first half of the nineteenth century were private companies and firefighters were fiercely proud of their units. They often competed like racing teams to see who could reach a blaze first. Tweed's company, named Americus, called themselves the "Tigers."

Firemen themselves were a daring, rowdy bunch, with competitive attitudes that sometimes led to violence. Tweed was dismissed from his job as foreman in 1850, when the Americus Tigers were accused of attacking members of another company with "axes, barrels, and missiles."

Firefighting in Old New York

As a member of New York City's volunteer fire department, William Tweed was part of a tradition dating back to 1737, when the Volunteer Department of the City of New York was established. The department began with a modest 35 men and two fire engines, but grew along with the metropolis.

New York City fire, 1850

In Tweed's day, bells were used to alert the volunteers that a blaze had started. From a number of watchtowers, volunteers kept a lookout for fires. When one was spotted, alarm bells were rung. The number of strokes of the bell told firefighters in which of the city's eight fire districts the fire was located. Firefighters would rush from wherever they were to answer the alarm; the men did not begin to live in firehouses until 1857.

Ironically, the corruption of the Tweed era helped bring about the demise of the volunteer fire department from which Boss Tweed had gotten his start. Citizens complained that their fire protection was inadequate; they stated that the volunteers were distracted from their duties by the fighting between companies. They also pointed out that embezzlement within the department, along with highly paid officers who received inflated salaries, together cost more than an entire force of professional firefighters would. In response to these complaints, in the spring of 1865 the state legislature established the Metropolitan Fire Department, a paid firefighting force.

In its heyday, however, New York's volunteer fire department was a potent political force. No fewer than seven volunteer firefighters went on to become mayor of New York City—and Boss Tweed rose from the ranks of the fire department to become the most powerful political figure the city had ever seen.

That fall, at age 27, Tweed ran for public office for the first time and won. Few who knew him were surprised at his political success. William Tweed was ideally suited for politics. With his outgoing personality, and the influence he acquired in his district while he was foreman of his firefighting company, Tweed had established himself as a natural grassroots leader who did not hesitate to get involved personally in the issues. Years later, when Tweed ran New York City almost singlehandedly, an English visitor described him as someone with "an abounding vitality, free and easy manners, plenty of humor—though of a coarse kind—and a jovial, swaggering way."

Tweed's first government office was as a city alderman, a legislator on the city council. After only two years in public service, he was elected to Congress. Service on a national level, however, did not suit him. Perhaps because he hailed from the bustling island of Manhattan, Tweed found Washington, D.C., to be little more than a boring backwater. Even though lawmakers at the time were wrestling with the weighty, high-profile issues of slavery and states' rights, Tweed had little interest in the nation outside of New York City. For him, the

THE HISTORY OF TAMMANY HALL

The Tammany Society was founded in 1789 by a group of Revolutionary War veterans. It was dedicated to the basic principles of the American Revolution, particularly the principle stated in the Declaration of Independence that "all men are created equal." As a charitable club, it helped the widows and orphaned children of men who had fought for the nation's independence.

Tammany was named after a legendary Delaware Indian chief, Tammanand. The club was governed by a board of "sachems"—a Native American term for chiefs—who dressed in Native American-inspired costumes for special ceremonies.

Although the Tammany Society was not originally a political organization, it quickly became one. This was partly due to the fact that the club was founded at the same time that New York City served as the capital of the United States. In March 1789, George Washington took his first oath of office at Federal Hall in New York City.

At that time, the nation's [...]

John Adams

20

ment, they believed, was necessary to hold together a nation of thirteen separate states. People who agreed with this point of view became known as Federalists. In many cases, the Federalists drew support from the wealthy classes—bankers, traders, and large landholders.

Opposing the Federalist point of view were people including Thomas Jefferson, the author of the Declaration of Independence and, eventually, the third president. Jefferson believed that most power should reside at the state and local level. He opposed a strong central government, and believed that democracy should be trusted to the people rather than to the leaders. Those who held this point of view became known as Jeffersonian Republicans—later they became Jeffersonian Democrats, then Democrats.

Thomas Jefferson

For the most part, these people came from the working class.

When John Adams was elected president in 1796, many Federalist bills were passed into law. One of the most controversial pieces of legislation passed during the Adams administration was the Alien and Sedition Acts. These acts increased from five to fourteen years the length of time an immigrant had to live in the United States before becoming a citizen. They also prohibited anyone from speaking out against the government—those who did faced fines and imprisonment. These laws angered Tammany members. Tammany Hall's change from a charity to a political organization was a result of the opposition of most of its members to the principles of the Federalists. The club members hated the Federalist policies of the Adams administration. They believed, with many other Americans, that the Alien and Sedition Acts violated the basic right of free speech that was guaranteed in the Bill of Rights. By 1800, Tammany Hall was recruiting men across New York City to vote against candidates of the Federalist Party, and Jefferson and his followers in the South had formed a bond with Tammany Hall.

One of the first sachems of Tammany Hall was Aaron Burr, who eventually served as vice president during Jefferson's first term and helped Democrats achieve victory. During the election campaign of 1800, Jefferson had met with Burr and Tammany leaders to form an anti-Federalist link between the workers in the East and small farmers in the South. On Election Day, Tammany Hall members organized and, in some cases,

Aaron Burr

paid voters to make sure that their supporters went to the polls to cast their ballots. The plan was so successful that Jefferson won, and Burr became his vice president.

Tammany Hall's strength as a political organization grew during the first decades of the 1800s. As Revolutionary War veterans died, Tammany's members came more and more from the working class. Almost all of these men supported the "common man" ideals of the newly named Democratic Party—and Tammany Hall.

In 1828, Democrat Andrew Jackson was elected president, thanks largely to the votes of workers in American cities. The leader of Tammany Hall, Martin Van Buren, helped Jackson run his campaign. When Jackson took office, he named Van Buren his secretary of state.

Van Buren was elected vice president during Jackson's second term and, in 1836, Tammany's leader was elected the president of the United States.

Jackson, Van Buren, and other Democrats strongly believed that any government job could be done by a person with average intelligence, rather than a wealthy aristocrat as had been the case up to that point. Following his beliefs, Jackson began the so-called "spoils system" and used his power to appoint party members to government jobs, from cabinet positions all the way down to postmaster in small rural communities.

This system of rewarding those who worked for a Democratic victory became the guiding principle in local politics. For Tammany Hall, that meant reaching out to New York's immigrants, offering jobs, food, and other services to newcomers. In return, Tammany asked for, and received, the immigrants' votes. Thus, in a city such as New York where the middle and upper classes had long held political power, Tammany and the common people gradually took control of city politics.

The combination of charity and spoils became an invitation to corruption. Tammany sachems began to buy the votes of the working class by offering money and jobs. They also bribed elected officials to vote for certain programs that would benefit them. By the time Bill Tweed joined Tammany Hall, the group—and its corrupt practices—was firmly entrenched within the political life in New York.

Martin Van Buren

thrill—and the benefit—of politics was strictly at the local level.

By the mid-1850s, Tweed had left Washington and returned to the rough-and-tumble New York City political scene. There, he used his considerable charm and leadership abilities to become a member of one of the most powerful political clubs in American history: Tammany Hall. It was a club with a rich legacy and, like Tweed, had been born right there in New York City.

In the mid-1850s, at the time Tweed became a member, Tammany Hall was a powerful Democratic political organization. Though Tammany had its roots in the Democratic principles of defending the rights of the so-called common man, by Tweed's time, the organization was evolving into a closely knit circle of self-serving political "buddies" who kept tight controls on the inner workings of New York City as a means of increasing their own interests.

Tammany Hall drew much of its political strength from a core constituency of recently arrived immigrants. The influx of these immigrants put great demands on the infrastructure of the city. New York had never before been faced wih the task of housing and assimilating such a mass of foreigners so quickly. As immigrants made up an increasing percentage of the city's population, their potential political power also grew. And, as their political power increased, so did the demand to address their needs.

Having cultivated his own following on a local level, Tweed was intrigued by the challenges of advancing his interests and bolstering influence through control of government. For this reason, Tammany Hall seemed the perfect place for the ambitious young politician. A native of the city, Tweed had grown up in the working-class neighborhoods of Manhattan, looking at wealth from the outside. He was thus able to use his understanding of the poor and disenfranchised to build his popularity and power among them. At the same time, he was a skillful and intelligent politician who knew how to use public approval for his personal benefit.

Chapter 3

A CITY GROWS, A BOSS RISES

In 1854, at the age of 31, Tweed accepted a post as commissioner of the board of education from the newly elected Democratic mayor—the first Democrat to hold the office. As commissioner, Tweed held considerable power. Among other things, he had approval over all building-and-supply contracts for schools. With such large budgets to play with, it did not take the new commissioner long to find ways of putting money in his pocket while handing contracts to fellow members of Tammany Hall. In 1857, Tweed was elected to the newly formed board of supervisors of the county of New York. During the following year, the members of this board began to acquire enormous fortunes from their control of the slow, costly construction of the city's premier project: the new county courthouse.

The corruption surrounding the construction was outrageous—and incredibly obvious. In 1858, its cost had been estimated at $350,000. After 12 years, the courthouse remained unfinished, yet it had cost the taxpayers of New York $13 million! Meanwhile, Tweed and his Tammany pals were enjoying luxuries and lavish lifestyles that would be out of reach for anyone living solely on the low city salaries allocated to the municipal positions they officially held.

As he amassed wealth through corruption during the years just before the Civil War, Tweed also took full advantage of his natural skills as a communicator. Utilizing his considerable persuasive abilities—and the huge amount of money under his control—Tweed began a public relations campaign that was aimed at enhancing his reputation and that of his cronies in city government. As he projected his larger-than-life image in public, he was also able to gain favor with the New York City newspapers by paying reporters to ensure that whatever the leaders of Tammany Hall did would receive favorable coverage in the press.

By the eve of the Civil War, Tweed had positioned himself as a kingpin in Tammany Hall. He might have solidified his control by 1860, if it had not been for a bitter division within the Democratic Party. In the presidential election of 1860, the issue of slavery almost brought an end to the party itself. Southern Democrats wanted to nominate a candidate who supported slavery in all states and territories. Northern Democrats wanted a candidate who would allow voters in each state and territory to decide for themselves the question of slavery.

Neither group favored the abolition of slavery. Their split was so deep, however, that the party nominated two men to run for president. The Southern Democrats nominated John C. Breckinridge, who was serving

John Breckinridge was nominated for president by the Southern Democrats in 1860.

as vice president under James Buchanan. The Northern Democrats nominated Illinois senator Stephen Douglas. Each took votes from the other, and the result was the election of Abraham Lincoln, an antislavery Republican. Within weeks after Lincoln's election, the first Southern states seceded. Even in the North, however, bitter feelings remained strong among the different Democratic factions. It fell to Tweed to try to unite the party as he rose higher in the ranks of Tammany Hall.

Stephen Douglas was nominated for president by the Northern Democrats in 1860.

In 1863, as the Civil War conflict was moving toward battlegrounds in Vicksburg, Mississippi, and Gettysburg, Pennsylvania, Tweed was faced with another major leadership challenge. During that summer, widespread violence erupted in the city. The riots began as a response to a military draft enacted in March 1863 by the federal government. The enormous number of

FREE SPEECH.
FREE HOMES.
FREE TERRITORY.

PROTECTION TO AMERICAN INDUSTRY

FOR PRESIDENT
ABRAHAM LINCOLN
OF ILLINOIS

FOR VICE PRESIDENT
HANNIBAL HAMLIN
OF MAINE

LITH. BY W.H. REASE

COR 4TH & CHESTNUT STS. PHILADA

Lincoln ran with Hannibal Hamlin in the election of 1860.

war casualties by that time had severely thinned the ranks of the Union army. President Lincoln, aware that his manpower advantage was slipping away, signed a law that required all men between the ages of 20 and 45 to register for service in the Union army. Names of those drafted would be selected by lottery.

The draft law exempted men in some occupations, such as telegraph operators, railroad engineers, judges, and certain other government employees.

A key provision of the law also allowed that—for the fee of $300—an eligible man could hire a substitute to serve for him.

Tweed was only 40 years old, but, as a city government employee, he was exempt from the draft. It soon became obvious to him, however, that the draft hit the working class the hardest. These people—who could not afford the $300 to hire replacements—formed the solid core of Tweed's supporters. Anger and resentment were fueled, in part, by poor timing. The first draftees from New York City

The Battle of Gettysburg—the bloodiest battle of the Civil War—occurred right before the draft was scheduled to begin in New York City.

were scheduled to be selected on July 12, 1863, a little more than a week after the Battle of Gettysburg, which was the bloodiest single battle in American history. The fighting had claimed thousands of New York lives among its 50,000 casualties. It was not a good time to institute a draft that would send thousands more New Yorkers to what many were convinced would be certain slaughter.

Before the draftees' names could be selected, a mob of mainly poor Irish workingmen went on a rampage in New York City. They burned down the draft office and killed militiamen, police officers, and

In 1863, draft riots destroyed property and claimed lives in New York City.

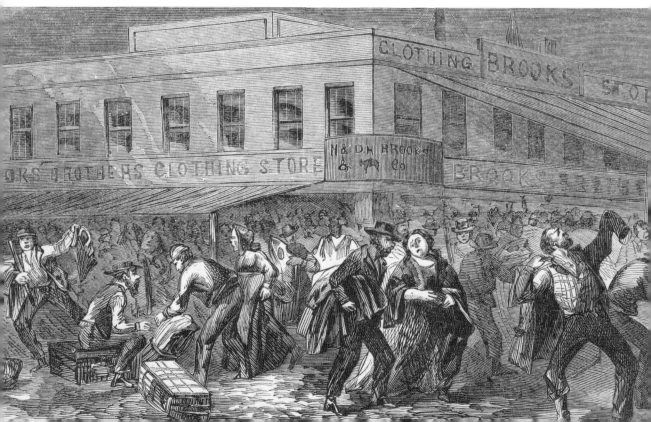

any African Americans they encountered. Although the violence began as a protest by poor citizens against the draft law, it soon turned into a revolt against the government in general. The riot, the worst in American history, lasted from July 13 to July 16. No one knows exactly how many people were killed in the violence, but estimates range from 100 to as many as 1,000. Blacks were lynched and beaten. Many buildings were burned to the ground, including a black church and a black orphanage, and numerous houses and stores were robbed and looted. Federal troops finally had to be called in to stop the fighting.

Though the violence had ended on the 16th, the anger of the rioters was ready to flare again at any moment. Tweed, hoping to prevent further bloodshed while he gained personal benefit, developed a plan to help his constituents. In one of his first actions as Grand Sachem, or leader, of Tammany Hall, he sponsored a low-interest loan program that granted men $300 to buy their way out of the draft. His efforts drew great praise from the poor neighborhoods of New York City, and he made a profit on the money he loaned.

Of course, Tweed was not the only person who used the war for his own benefit. Among the men who paid a substitute to fight in his place was a young oil company owner named John D. Rockefeller. Freed from military service, Rockefeller began to build his oil company into one of the most profitable businesses in the United States. Over the last half of the nineteenth century, he amassed one of the world's greatest fortunes.

On April 9, 1865, Confederate general Robert E. Lee and Union commander Ulysses S. Grant met at a private home in Appomattox Court House, Virginia. In one of the final acts of the Civil War, Grant wrote out the terms of surrender for Lee's Army of Northern Virginia, and Lee signed the document. The long, brutal war was over.

Across the North, there was celebration. In New York City, bells pealed, guns roared, and fireworks exploded to mark the occasion. Soldiers, firemen, sailors, judges, professors, and politicians all draped themselves in red, white, and blue to parade down city streets. As the newly anointed leader of city politics, William "Boss" Tweed led the victory parade in New York City.

Appomattox Court House, Virginia, was the setting for Lee's surrender to Grant, which effectively ended the Civil War.

A week later, the same city streets—and most streets in the North—were draped in black. President Abraham Lincoln had been assassinated by a pro-South radical named John Wilkes Booth. The United States had won a war but lost a leader. Without the calming and rational leadership of Lincoln, the unification process became more difficult. It took decades to heal the national wounds caused by the Civil War.

At a meeting of Tammany Hall, the most powerful Democratic organization in the nation, Tweed mourned the death of the beloved Republican president. Lincoln, said Tweed in his eulogy, had been "called away by an assassin's hand at the time he appeared the only person who could safely navigate the nation once again upon the path of freedom and once again unite us."

On April 24, two weeks after the joyous end-of-war parade, Lincoln's body arrived in New York on the way to its final resting place in Illinois. A funeral procession wound slowly down Broadway, past silent crowds of mourners. The only sounds were the steady tolling of the bells and the muffled beat of drums. The next day, the coffin was carried to the Hudson River Railway depot. Along with other members of the city government, William Tweed marched behind the funeral hearse that was drawn by sixteen horses.

An Era of Growth

Lincoln's death cast a shadow across much of the North. By the end of 1865, however, peace had brought new energy to the nation. Now there was

President Lincoln's funeral procession makes its way down Pennsylvania Avenue in Washington, D.C., 1865.

work to be done. Across the country, Americans built factories, laid rail lines, settled land, mined coal, and established colleges. An era of economic growth unlike any in the nation's history had begun.

By this time, Tweed and his close adviser, parks commissioner Peter Sweeny, had taken complete control of Tammany Hall politics. Not only was Tweed's circle controlling New York City politics, they were also working closely with the Democratic National Committee and national party leaders. The nomination of Governor Horatio Seymour to oppose Ulysses Grant in the presidential election of 1868 was held in a luxurious new Tammany Hall building, which was completed just in time to host the delegates. Tweed came through for his candidate by insuring that New York carried Seymour in the election, even though Grant won the larger contest. By 1869, the New York state legislature won a Democratic majority for the first time in twenty years. With fellow Tammany-backed Democrats in place in Albany—ones who controlled and approved the finances for the city—Tweed was perfectly positioned to exploit his power and influence in nearly every corner of the state.

This cartoon by Thomas Nast shows the four "kingpins" of city government: Tweed, Sweeny, Hall, and Connolly.

Chapter 4

DAWN OF THE GILDED AGE

*A*s the 1860s came to an end, a spirit of optimism had replaced the gloom of war in many parts of the country. Most people in the North believed wholeheartedly in the so-called American Dream— that with hard work, anyone could get rich. Much of this optimism was fueled by a boom in manufacturing and the widespread growth of factories. These key elements of industry had, in turn, been supported by the recent surge in the immigrant population. More immigrants meant more cheap labor. And cheap labor meant bigger profits and, thus, more production.

A group of sightseers listens to a tour guide in New York City in the late 1800s.

The Growth of Cities

One aspect of the Gilded Age that set it apart from other eras was the enormous growth of cities during the period. In 1800, only six cities in the United States had more than 8,000 people living in them. By 1860, 1 out of 6 Americans lived in a city of more than 10,000 people. By 1900, 1 in 3 did. Cities boomed in the Northeast, along the Great Lakes, and on the Pacific Coast. "We cannot all live in cities," wrote the well-known newspaper publisher Horace Greeley. "Yet nearly all seem determined to do so."

New York City, perhaps more than any other city, exemplified the new American metropolis. At the close of the Civil War, New York City was just shy of 700,000 people. This estimate—which shocked many New Yorkers as incredibly high— was reached after the tabulations of a single clerk were checked, re-done, and re-tabulated. With the news of the city's increased size came a new sense of urgency—the sense that a vastly improved infrastructure was going to be needed to accommodate the burgeoning population.

During the 1860s and early 1870s, New York City streets were filled with garbage, animal waste, and mud.

New York, like many other growing urban centers, was a study in sharp contrasts. On one hand, it had grown into the business, financial, and artistic capital of the nation. On the other hand, it was, overall, a poor city—and poorly run. Sewage systems were practically nonexistent. There were no programs for public sanitation. Waste from horse-drawn carts filled the streets. The stench from slaughterhouses, rotting garbage, decaying animals, and manufacturing fouled the air from one end of the island to the other.

Jane Addams founded Hull House in Chicago to help the city's poor and struggling population.

Other cities with rapidly expanding immigrant communities faced similar problems. Like New York, urban centers such as Chicago and Pittsburgh suffered problems created by too many people crowded into a desperately limited living space. New citizens from foreign lands often faced fear and prejudice from those who had already settled in a neighborhood. This fear heightened tensions and sometimes led to violence between people of different ethnic and cultural backgrounds.

Primitive sanitation systems and inefficient garbage collection bred diseases such as cholera, typhus, and typhoid. In one Chicago slum, more than half of all infants died before reaching age one. Pickpockets and thieves roamed the streets. There were no hydrants on the streets, or sprinkler systems in townhouses and apartment buildings. Fire was a constant danger—a blaze in one building could easily level an entire block.

Municipal governments offered little or no help with these problems in New York City. Unlike today, when most of a city's major needs are administered by a central city government—or city hall—New York in the mid-to-late 1800s was a jumble of unconnected communities, independent businesses, and disparate interests. No central authority existed to oversee the development or maintenance of the city's infrastructure. It was, for all intents and purposes, urban chaos.

William "Boss" Tweed had a plan to lead New York out of this chaos. His leadership (though iron-handed and self-serving) for the first time brought some sense of unity to city government. The form of unity he provided was certainly flawed, but—at the time—it was the only unity the city had ever known. Many citizens shared the view that some unity was better than none, no matter what the shortcomings. The new boss also knew how to make people happy.

For example, he had learned in numerous instances—especially the draft riots—that monetary pay-offs are a highly persuasive and effective way to make others cooperate. To unite the city's print media, Tweed paid regular stipends to influential reporters on each of the city's most prominent newspapers in return for favorable coverage. He also paid reporters in out-of-town journals to write favorable stories about New York City government. These "bought" stories would then be reprinted in New York papers. Tweed's highly successful "pay-off principle" continued to guide his strategy as he took increasing control of New York City from the inside.

Tweed was also a master influence-peddler. Charismatic and self-assured, he enlisted cohorts by appealing to their base desires for money and power. He also allowed people who cooperated to do as they pleased within their own domains. The board of education, under his direction, allowed teachers in predominantly Catholic neighborhoods to ignore the Protestant-based rituals that had been in place previously. Police officers who worked deals with liquor distributors were allowed to "look the other way" when liquor was illegally sold on Sunday.

✒ HORATIO ALGER'S AMERICA ✒

One of the most widely read authors of the late 1800s was a New York City clergyman named Horatio Alger. From 1866 until Alger's death in 1897, his novels, such as *Ragged Dick*, *Luck and Pluck*, and *Fame and Fortune*, sold hundreds of thousands of copies. The theme of each book was the same: honesty and hard work lead to success—and success in that era meant great wealth. Today, someone whose life is described as a "Horatio Alger story" is a person who has worked hard to overcome obstacles and achieve success.

Although his writing and his themes might seem corny to modern readers, Alger was among the most popular authors of his time—in some ways, he was the literary voice of the Gilded Age. Alger's message that wealth equaled success became almost a religious belief among Americans. Making money became more than a goal—it became a crusade that motivated everyone from shopkeepers to multi-millionaires. As the president of Temple University in Philadelphia told his students at graduation ceremonies, "I say that you ought to get rich, and it is your duty to get rich. To make money honestly is to preach the gospel."

Within this atmosphere, William Tweed enjoyed his leading role in New York City politics. Though he was already prominent and powerful by 1866, he was at his height in 1869, when he won state election.

Horatio Alger

The Age of Democratization

The tidal wave of immigration that hit America's shores late in the nineteenth century forever changed the face of the nation. It affected daily life on nearly every level. It created new neighborhoods, made new goods and services available, and significantly changed the political mix of city populations—and the country as a whole. This shift in political objectives—the new demand to serve the needs of hundreds of thousands of working men and women—defined the political evolution of America in the Gilded Age. The nineteenth century had become the era of democratization. Sheer numbers dictated a new sense of power for the so-called common people. The old trappings of rigid class structures and hierarchies were rejected in favor of a new respect and acknowledgement of the important roles played by American laborers.

Boss Tweed was keenly aware of the political shifts that were occurring all around him. And, in those shifts, he saw opportunity. As the middle- and working-class population became more visible, sharp contrasts between America's super-rich and super-poor became more obvious.

The contrasts of the Gilded Age were most glaring in New York City. In the second half of the nineteenth century, it became the nation's most important city— the greatest seaport, the greatest railway center, and the greatest shopping center, as well as the center of industry and finance. "Not London, not Paris, not Moscow," one New Yorker boasted, "can now surpass the future certainties of the thirteen-mile island of Manhattan."

At the same time, however, New York City was home to more than 1 million people by 1870—and nearly half of them (44%) were poor immigrants. Of that immigrant population, 21% had been born in Ireland, and 16% had been born in Germany. The vast majority could neither read nor write. As the population exploded, immigrants suffered from overcrowded living conditions. By 1890, two-thirds of New York's population lived in tenements—musty, sunless, and disease-ridden buildings. Many tenements had no heat or running water.

As early as 1872, writer Charles Brace described the desperate living conditions in New York. In a report on one tenement he wrote: "In a dark cellar filled with smoke, there sleep, all in one room, with

By 1870, nearly half of New York City's population was made up of poor immigrants.

no kind of partition dividing them, two men with their wives, a girl of thirteen or fourteen, two men and a large boy of about seventeen years of age, a mother with two more boys, one about ten years old and one large boy of fifteen; another women with two boys, nine and eleven years of age—in all fourteen persons."

A decade later, novelist William Dean Howells admitted that from a distance, a tenement might not seem so bad. "But to be in it, and not have the distance, is to inhale the stenches of the neglected street, and to catch the . . . poverty-smell which breathes from the open doorways."

BOSS TWEED AND TAMMANY HALL

Twain Names the Gilded Age

In the early 1870s, the legendary American writer Mark Twain focused on the national craze for wealth—but he gave it his own uniquely satirical twist. Living in the booming industrial city of Hartford, Connecticut, he wrote a witty novel called *The Gilded Age*. Its main character, "Colonel" Beriah Sellers, is full of get-rich-quick schemes. One of his plans is to manufacture a fake medicine, "Sellers' Infallible Imperial Oriental Optic Lineament and Salvation for Sore Eyes." The first year, he explains to a friend, he might sell 55,000 bottles. "The second year sales would reach 200,000 bottles. . . . The third year we could easily sell one million bottles in the United States. . . . Three years of introducing trade in the Orient and what will be the result? Annual income—well, God knows how many millions and millions apiece!"

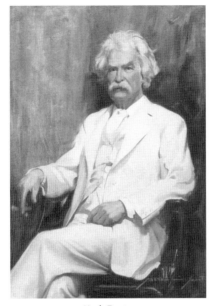

Mark Twain

Twain's portrait of conniving businessmen rang so true that the title of his book was applied to the whole era. Today, the era's name refers specifically to the years between 1866 and 1900, during which some of the greatest fortunes in American history were made.

Tammany Helps the Poor

Beginning in the middle of the nineteenth century, Tammany Hall was one of the few charitable or political organizations that helped the city's workers and poorest inhabitants. There were no unemployment or welfare laws and no government agencies to which people could turn for assistance. From loans to jobs to housing, Tammany Hall took care of the common people.

Although the local politicians were helpful, Tammany's members did not offer assistance solely from the goodness of their hearts. In return for financial assistance, the organization expected political support. Tammany political leader George Plunkitt explained the Tammany attitude: "Think what the people of New York are. One half, more than one half, are of foreign birth. They do not speak our language, they do not know our laws, they are the raw material with which we have to build up the state. . . . There is no denying the service that Tammany has rendered the Republic. There is no other organization for taking hold of untrained, friendless men and converting them into citizens. Who else in the city would do it?"

Having built his career on a local level in New York City, Tweed understood the give-and-take nature of local politics. Thus, when he became the Grand Sachem of Tammany Hall, he was able to call on various groups—such as the Catholic Church and the labor unions—to assist in his programs and make them appear more legitimate. Working with those groups, Tweed and Tammany Hall raised funds to build hospitals, almshouses, and orphanages. They helped support public and parochial schools. They found jobs for the unemployed. Tammany Hall handed out turkeys at Thanksgiving and coal at Christmas. Their public efforts were widely praised in New York. In exchange, grateful recipients flocked to the polls on Election Day and voted the way Tammany wanted them to.

Tweed also built public support for his efforts to gain political power in less obvious ways. Using his influence, Tweed brought other members of Tammany Hall into city government. These men formed the so-called Tweed Ring: Peter "Brains" Sweeny, the city treasurer; Richard "Slippery Dick" Connolly, the city comptroller; and Mayor Abraham Oakey Hall. In 1860, the Ring pushed through a

Abraham Hall was mayor of New York City in the early 1860s.

new city charter that allowed them to control the city treasury. Incredibly, every bill submitted to the city was increased by 50%, and all the additional money went to Tweed and his friends.

Despite the corruption and self-serving politics that characterized the Tweed years, the city enjoyed many tangible and sorely needed improvements during this time. In fact, public programs for municipal renovations virtually poured from Tammany Hall. Huge projects that involved the improvement of the city's docks, piers, and waterfront avenues were begun. Wide-scale upgrades were made to the sewage system, water supply, system, bridges, and streets. Tammany even offered a city-subsidized

This political cartoon accuses the Tweed Ring of inflating city contracts so money can go into the pockets of Tammany members.

program that helped private homeowners refurbish their homes. Tweed and his allies won support in high and respectable circles with their motto "something for everyone."

City government also became better organized during this period. Before 1870, New York's streets were controlled by three different and independent sets of officials. After 1870, Mayor Abraham Hall—a Tweed Ring insider—made a major plea to centralize all the city's major commissions, and to concentrate authority under one person who would oversee all the major departments of public works. That person was, needless to say, Boss Tweed, superintendent of public works.

As superintendent of public works, Tweed was in charge of most city development projects. For the Boss, political programs and personal interests went hand in hand. The money gained from padding the bills was divided into five parts. Tweed, Sweeny, Hall and Connolly each received one part, and the fifth part went toward bribes.

Connecting Cities to Cities

The accelerated growth that New York City experienced in the 1860s and 1870s was caused by a combination of factors that all came together at just the right time. A huge influx of immigrants. Improved manufacturing technology. A growth in factories.

CORRUPTION: A NATIONAL EPIDEMIC

The Gilded Age was, indeed, an optimistic era when many a man made his fortune through hard work and innovation. Anything that is gilded, however, shines only on the surface. There was also a dark underside to this age of wealth. In politics, corruption had taken hold at nearly every level, from local to national. While the Tweed Ring wielded enormous power in New York City, other city bosses and their rings became fantastically wealthy in cities such as Philadelphia, Pittsburgh, Boston, and Chicago. Such widespread corruption, however, was not limited to local governments.

At the national level, the bitter impeachment and trial of President Andrew Johnson in 1867—the first in American history—left many Americans deeply disappointed in elected officials. In 1868, hoping for a change in Washington,

Ulysses S. Grant

Americans elected war hero Ulysses S. Grant to the presidency. As tough as he was on the battlefield, however, Grant was an inept administrator who had a soft spot for political cronies. As a result, his eight years in office have long been regarded as two of the most corrupt terms in American history.

Many of the people Grant appointed to White House jobs took advantage of their positions in order to steal money. The most notorious episode was the Crédit Mobilier Scandal of 1872. At that time, shortly before Grant ran for re-election to a second term, it was revealed that many high-level politicians—including Schuyler Colfax, Grant's own vice president—had been bribed by the Crédit Mobilier Corporation in order to obtain the rights to build the Transcontinental Railroad.

Another reason for the city's tremendous expansion was the improvement of national transportation networks. These networks allowed goods to be shipped more easily and inexpensively to and from America's key cities. The Erie Canal had made a significant impact in this regard by 1825. By 1869, however, an even more extensive transportation system connected the nation's East Coast with the West Coast, and opened up huge commercial shipping routes that had never before existed.

The Transcontinental Railroad

In 1860, more than 70% of all railroads were located in the Northern states. In 1863, work on a national project began to change all that. It was the construction of a transcontinental railroad that was to connect the East and West Coasts.

On May 10, 1869, two construction teams met at Promontory Point in Utah. The president of the Union Pacific Railroad hammered a golden spike into the rail where the two lines met. It was engraved with these words: "May God continue the unity of our Country as the Railroad unites the two great Oceans of the world."

The two ends of the Transcontinental Railroad met in Promontory Point, Utah, in 1869.

Over the next decade, many other long-distance rail lines were built. The Atchison, Topeka, and the Santa Fe went from Chicago to Santa Fe and on to Southern California. The Great Northern linked St. Paul and Seattle. The rise of railroads enabled factories and farms to send goods almost anywhere

Rail travel had changed daily life in America by the 1870s.

in the United States. By the end of the 1870s, New York could buy beef shipped from Chicago, wheat shipped from the Midwest, steel made in Pennsylvania, and textiles made in Massachusetts or South Carolina. America went from being a nation of isolated small farms and towns to a nation of interconnected cities and towns.

BOSS TWEED AND TAMMANY HALL

While the rise of railroads was a great benefit to most Americans, it was an even greater benefit to the men who controlled the railroad companies. Fortunes were built from acquiring ownership of a profitable railroad and then selling pieces of the company—called shares or stocks—to investors. This link between industry and finance built most of the greatest fortunes of the Gilded Age.

Many of the fortunes of the time, however, were not built by entirely honest financial dealings. New York City's wealthiest investors called on Tammany Hall to make sure their railroad-related investments and other ventures remained unhindered by city officials. Tweed, for example, was instrumental in defusing a battle between two of New York's most powerful financiers, Jay Gould and Cornelius Vanderbilt, who were competing for control of the Erie Railroad in 1868. Although Gould fared best in that battle (and returned the favor by getting Tweed elected to the Erie board of directors and promising him support from all the counties along the railroad's route), the Boss soon pulled strings for Vanderbilt. When landowners demanded that the tracks of Vanderbilt's New York and Harlem River Railroad be covered, Tweed intervened by forcing a compromise and successfully demanding that the city pay half of Vanderbilt's costs.

Such corrupt partnerships between city officials and financiers were not unique to New York City. Federal officials were no more immune to corruption and graft than their municipal counterparts. In 1877, for example, Collis Huntington, a wealthy railroad tycoon, explained the way he did business in Washington, D.C. "If you have to pay money [to a politician] to have the right thing done, it is only just and fair to do it.... If a [politician] ... won't do right unless he is bribed to do it, I think... it is a man's duty to go up and bribe."

The Rise of Corporations

As railroad companies built more lines, they formed rail networks crisscrossing the United States. Soon large railroad companies began buying smaller ones. The Pennsylvania Railroad, for example, was a combination of 73 smaller railroads. This practice led to the formation of corporations. These corporations sold stocks to investors to acquire large amounts of cash, which was then used to buy up smaller corporations.

JAY GOULD, TWEED CRONY

Just as William Tweed came to symbolize the big-city boss, there was no better example of the robber baron than his crony, Jay Gould. Born into poverty in upstate New York, Gould rose from a series of menial jobs to become a surveyor, then a tannery operator, and then a leather merchant. With savings that he had amassed over the years, he eventually began speculating in railroads. By the time he was in his early thirties, he had become a director of the Erie Railroad.

As a railroad director, Gould honed his already-notorious unscrupulous business skills. To thwart a takeover attempt by Cornelius Vanderbilt, Gould and his allies on the Erie board of directors sold illegal Erie shares and bribed state lawmakers to pass legislation favorable to them. Once the threat from Vanderbilt had been eliminated, Gould and his cohorts, including Tweed, proceeded to plunder the railroad in much the same way that the Tweed Ring looted the public treasury of New York City.

Railroad fortunes were not enough for Gould. In 1869, he and others bought large amounts of gold—which rapidly raised the price—with the intention of selling it at a profit when the price became high enough. The plan failed when the government released enough gold to drive the price back down, but it also provoked a financial panic and widespread public outrage. As a result, Gould was forced from the Erie Railroad in 1872, not long after the demise of the Tweed Ring.

Jay Gould

Gould, however, ultimately fared better than Tweed. With a large fortune, he began to invest in railroads in the West, and became a director of the Union Pacific railroad in 1874. He then proceeded to build his own railroad empire, and, at his death in 1892, he left to his sons a fortune estimated at nearly $80 million.

John D. Rockefeller built an empire in the oil business.

Soon, corporations formed groups called trusts, which controlled entire industries. Trusts that grow so large that they control entire industries are known as monopolies. Eventually, the Gilded Age became an era ruled economically by large monopolies, particularly those in oil, steel, and railroads. These monopolies attempted to destroy competition in whatever industry they controlled. Oil tycoon John D. Rockefeller and steel tycoon Andrew Carnegie, for example, oversaw monopolies that bought, undersold, or otherwise ruined any businesses they saw as competition.

The monopolies that arose during the Gilded Age were in keeping with other centralized, unregulated, all-powerful organizations that had come to rule American life. The rise of monopolies was allowed because economists—and politicians—at that time were against government regulation of industry. They believed that competition was fairest without government interference. As a result, the federal government allowed businesses—and personal fortunes—to grow without any oversight from the government.

Andrew Carnegie built his fortune with steel.

The complete lack of government regulation also affected workers. Nineteenth-century Americans were so opposed to any regulation that their labor laws fell short of those of every other industrialized nation. Workplace safety, child labor, work hours, and other issues were ignored. Despite the enormous power of monopolies and the corporate lack of sympathy for workers, there was no national agreement in the late 1800s about how to end unfair business practices.

THE NOTORIOUS "ROBBER BARONS"

Over the course of the four decades between 1860 and 1900, the Gilded Age produced billionaires whose names are well known even today. John D. Rockefeller's fortune was built on oil; Andrew Carnegie's was built on steel. Most fortunes made in those years, however, were made in the construction and operation of the 200,000 miles of railroad track that spread across the United States like a great steel web.

The men who built vast fortunes during the Gilded Age came to be known as "robber barons." This nickname suggests the ambivalence with which they were viewed: on one hand, they were "barons" of great wealth who seemingly had achieved the American dream of success. On the other hand, they achieved that wealth by stealing from others— forcing their competitors out of business and paying workers low wages.

Perhaps the most notorious of the new breed of Gilded Age businessmen was New York native Cornelius Vanderbilt (1794-1877). Like many men who built fortunes during this period, Vanderbilt was propelled by nearly superhuman energy and motivated by an iron-willed determination to succeed. "I have been insane on the subject of moneymaking all my life," he once said. Born into a poor family on Staten Island, New York, young Vanderbilt borrowed $100 from his mother when he was 16 and started a passenger ferry business to Manhattan.

Cornelius Vanderbilt

He soon expanded his fleet up the Hudson. By the 1830s, the "Commodore," as he was called, had turned to the brand-new steamship business, which he gradually dominated by undercutting his competitors and introducing luxury to travel. By the 1840s, Vanderbilt had more than 100 steamboats carrying passengers and goods along the East Coast and up the Hudson.

Always on the lookout for a good investment, Vanderbilt decided after the Civil War that railroads were a certain moneymaker. He began buying up railroad lines. By the time of his death, he controlled the railroad route between New York and Chicago. Every time he bought a company, he put someone else out of business. The *New York Times* first used the term "robber baron" to describe Vanderbilt.

When Cornelius Vanderbilt died, he left all of his fortune to his son William, who inherited his father's arrogant attitude as well as his money. After William canceled a mail train and someone asked how the loss would affect the public, he replied, "The public be damned."

Another of the legendary robber barons was Andrew Carnegie (1835-1919). Born in Scotland, Carnegie came to America at age 12 and went to work in a Pennsylvania cotton mill for $1.20 a week. A year later he acquired a job as a messenger boy at a nearby telegraph office and soon made himself an indispensable worker.

Carnegie's rags-to-riches tale really started one day when he found a check for $500 on the street and turned it in. Much impressed, a Pittsburgh newspaper reporter wrote a story about the "honest little fellow." A local railroad executive read it and decided to hire Andy as his telegraph operator. The ambitious boy had already taught himself Morse code, and Carnegie's rise began. Once he was making a good salary, Carnegie invested his money in trains, railroad bridges, and oil derricks.

By age 33, Andrew Carnegie was a rich man. But his biggest deals were yet to come. Convinced that steel was the building material of the future, Carnegie built a modern steel plant outside Pittsburgh, Pennsylvania. The plant used a faster, cheaper method of purifying iron to make Bessemer steel. The new metal was lighter and stronger than iron and bent rather than breaking, making it perfect for construction.

Soon railroad companies began to buy high-quality Bessemer steel from Carnegie for their rails. The huge profits he made enabled Carnegie to buy out his steelmaking competition. By purchasing warehouses, iron mines, and railroad lines, he gained control of all the steps in the steelmaking process, from mining ore to shipping the finished product.

Carnegie's philosophy matched the mood of the Gilded Age perfectly. He believed that successful businessmen had

Cambria Steelworks, Johnstown, Pennsylvania, 1876

both the right and the duty to make as much money as possible. "The millionaires . . . are the bees that make the most honey, and contribute most to the hive even after they have gorged themselves," he asserted. But Carnegie also thought the rich had the responsibility to donate their money where it would do the most good.

Perhaps the best-known robber baron of the era was John D. Rockefeller (1839-1937). Rockefeller grew up in Cleveland, Ohio, where his mother taught him to be hardworking, efficient, and thrifty. When oil was discovered in the hills of western Pennsylvania in 1859, Rockefeller was one of the first to recognize its moneymaking possibilities. He bought his way out of military service in the Civil War, and invested in his first refinery to purify oil for kerosene.

As Rockefeller's business grew, he began to buy up the competition, often by unfair means. In some cases, he got lower shipping costs for his oil by getting railroad companies to give him a kickback, called a rebate, every time he used their lines. He also forced shipping companies to charge other oil companies more to ship their oil, which caused those oil companies to lose money. At the first sign of a competitor's weakness, Rockefeller closed in and bought the company. By 1880, Rockefeller's corporation, the Standard Oil Company of Ohio, controlled the oil business in America and became one of the most notorious monopolies in the country.

The Gap Between Rich and Poor

During the heady days of the Gilded Age, brilliant, ruthless men such as the robber barons made millions for themselves—and their industries helped push America to the top of the world's economic ladder. By cutting off competition and keeping costs down, they also made it possible for people to buy products at lower prices.

In order to make money, however, the robber barons had to pay extremely low wages to their

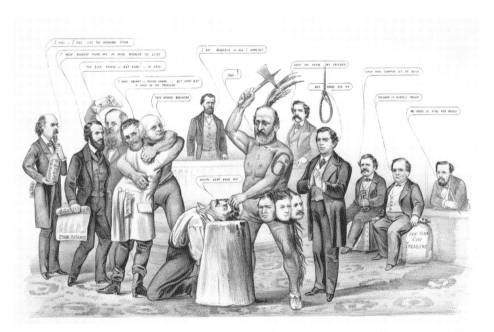

Tweed was known for his tight—sometimes brutal—control of Tammany Hall, as this cartoon illustrates.

workers. Though wealth was created through the labor of millions, it filled just a few pockets. The glaring contrasts between rich and poor were everywhere. Writer Hamlin Garland, visiting one of Carnegie's steel towns, wrote, "The streets were horrible; the buildings poor; the sidewalks sunken and full of holes. . . . Everywhere the yellow mud of the streets lay kneaded into sticky masses through which groups of pale, lean men slouched in faded garments."

While workers existed in poverty, millionaires spent conspicuously. They bought gilded furniture, crystal chandeliers, 120-foot yachts—even cigarettes wrapped in $100 dollar bills and oysters decorated with black pearls. What, if anything, could be done to close the vast gap between rich and poor? The workers of New York City turned to Tammany Hall and Boss Tweed for the answer.

Chapter 5

THE FALL OF
THE TWEED RING

By the winter of 1871, Boss Tweed was at the height of his power and wealth. He lived in a mansion on Fifth Avenue, had a weekend estate in Connecticut, owned a private yacht, and drove a carriage with gold-plated harnesses on the horses. At the marriage of his daughter Mary Amelia, one newspaper reported that he wore "a diamond like a planet in his shirt front." The young man from Cherry Street had come a long way since his days as the foreman of the Americus Tigers firefighters.

Although Tweed was now at the pinnacle of his power, the administration he oversaw had begun to show signs of faltering. People—even Tweed's most loyal supporters—could not help noticing that something was amiss. Between 1868 and 1870, the city

Communication in Tweed's Day

Today, it seems unbelievable that Boss Tweed's misdeeds went unnoticed for so long by most ordinary citizens of New York City. Yet, in Tweed's day, the city—and communication within it—was very different from what it is today.

New York in the mid-nineteenth century was a sprawling metropolis that had sprouted up with little, if any, formal planning. Main thoroughfares often followed paths that had been used by Native Americans long before Europeans arrived. Not only was the layout convoluted and twisting, the streets were perpetually in poor shape—muddy, congested, and choked with refuse. Because these conditions made the streets difficult to navigate, most New Yorkers rarely ventured far from their own neighborhoods. This lack of mobility meant that many people had no way of learning about events that were happening right across town. A lack of communication technology meant that there was also no easy way to communicate with someone in another neighborhood.

Although the telegraph was in widespread use by Tweed's day, the messages it carried had to be transmitted in Morse code. This was most effective in sending short, urgent messages—not lengthy, descriptive ones. Mailing letters or making telephone calls were not options—the postal service was highly unreliable within the city, and the telephone had yet to be invented.

Newspapers were not a dependable source of local information either. Although New York boasted more than 20 daily papers, their pages were usually filled with out-of-town news that came from wire services and press associations. News from wire services was less expensive to obtain than local news gathered by reporters who had to be paid individually. Even when the papers did report local news, it was often biased. Considering all these factors, it is clear that the primitive state of communication in nineteenth-century New York helped Tweed to go about his business unnoticed for as long as he did.

debt increased by more than $30 million. "The spectacle is appalling," poet Walt Whitman, a New York City native, wrote in 1871. "The official services . . . are saturated in corruption, bribery, falsehood, and maladministration . . . robbery and scoundrelism."

By 1870, forces were at work to destroy Tweed. Illustrator Thomas Nast published numerous cartoons attacking Tweed and his Ring. As he had done throughout his career, Tweed tried to use a bribe to fix his problem. He offered Nast $500,000—an incredible sum in those days—to go to Europe and to stop drawing his editorial cartoons. Nast, however, turned the Boss down.

"I don't think I'll do it," Nast replied. "I made up my mind not long ago to put some of these fellows behind bars, and I'm going to put them there."

As concern mounted over the city's financial stability, Tweed's enemies began enlisting support. They worked behind the scenes as Nast's cartoons helped to turn public opinion against Tweed. The anti-Tweed *New York Times* continued to print editorials that exposed and denounced the evils of Tammany Hall. Initially, these efforts had little effect. Tweed controlled the city government so closely that

This Nast cartoon appeared in Harper's Weekly *in August 1871, as the Tweed Ring crumbled. It depicts members of the Ring trying to blame each other for their wrongdoing.*

there was no physical proof of wrongdoing. Nast and the newspapers were forced to rely on hearsay, rumors, and allegations, albeit from reliable sources.

By the spring of 1871, rumors about the dangerous size of New York City's debt and excessive borrowing began to circulate. Investors and foreign financiers took note of this, and instantly ceased all investment in the city.

A twist of fate finally brought Tweed and his Ring down. Unfortunately for Tweed, James Watson, the city auditor, had been thrown from his sleigh and fatally injured in the winter of 1870. He was replaced by an associate of James O'Brien, a political enemy of Tweed's. The new auditor soon gathered top-secret and highly incriminating documentation of city and county accounts.

O'Brien offered the "scoop" to Tweed's archenemy, the *New York Times*. When Tweed and his men learned that *Times* had this information, they offered the publisher George Jones an enormous $5 million bribe not to publish it. Jones refused the bribe, and, on July 8, 1871, the paper ran the first in a series of damning articles that recounted a long list of frauds and crimes that had been perpetrated upon the city.

On July 29, 1871, the *Times* published 200,000 copies of a four-page summary of all of the information provided to it by the new county auditor. Among many things, the report showed that, in the four years between 1867 and 1871, the city's indebtedness had tripled, from $30 million to $90 million. Two-thirds of that increase was contracted between 1869 and 1871. New Yorkers were astonished to see how their money had been misspent. For the new county courthouse project alone, eleven thermometers had cost the city

$7,500. Dust brooms came to $41,000. One contractor had been paid $5.69 million for carpets, window shades, and furniture. Altogether, the courthouse had cost four times as much as London's Houses of Parliament and twice as much as the purchase of Alaska. Even more astonishing was the fact that, twelve years after construction had begun, the building was still not completed.

The need for reform was now urgent. Upon the publication of the *Times* articles, New York's credit was effectively frozen by the banks. Without credit, the city would not be able to make its next interest payment of $2.7 million, due on November 1, just six days before the next election.

On September 4, 1871, New York's political leaders held a reform meeting. There, a so-called Committee of Seventy was appointed to prosecute Tweed and take down the Tammany Hall Ring. Henry Stebbins, banker and former president of the Central Park Commission, was elected chairman of the new committee. Stebbins was appointed to lead the high level attack, along with the head of the state Democratic committee, Samuel Tilden, and the national party chairman, August Belmont. Tilden,

The Poison Pen of Thomas Nast

As a boy on the Lower East Side of New York, Thomas Nast (1840-1902) loved watching the red fire trucks that raced up and down the city streets. When the bell clanged, he grabbed his pencil and paper and rushed outside to sketch all the excitement. He especially admired one dashing young fireman, Bill Tweed. Years later, Nast would become disillusioned with his one-time hero—and help to destroy him.

Nast's artistic talent had been obvious from the time he moved from Germany to the United States at age six. When he was just 22, he was already a correspondent on the battlefields of the Civil War, sending eyewitness drawings back to the magazine

Thomas Nast

Harper's Weekly. Nast had a sharp wit and a great interest in politics. Although he conducted his most famous campaign against the Tweed Ring, many politicians were the target of his sharp pen. It was Nast who created those two lasting political symbols, the Democratic donkey and Republican elephant. He has long been recognized as the most influential cartoonist ever in American politics. Nast's most famous contribution to American culture, however, was a fat, jolly elf with a full white beard and a red suit.

Drawing on an image he remembered from his German childhood, Thomas Nast created the image of Santa Claus we know today.

Samuel Tilden headed the New York State Democratic Committee in the early 1870s.

who had plans to run for the presidency, knew that he had to distance himself as soon as possible from Tweed's administration, which he considered a "black mark" on the Democratic Party. "I fear," Tilden said, "that the impression will be spread throughout the country that the evils and abuses in the local government in the city of New York are general characteristics of the Democratic Party and would occur in the Federal government if that party should come into power in Washington."

After the September 4 meeting, a quick-moving plan was set in motion. On September 7, an injunction was issued that restrained the comptroller or any other official from spending any money. The reaction within Tammany Hall was panic. Offices were ransacked, records were destroyed, and the cover-ups began. By mid-October, the Tweed Ring was nearing extinction. Tilden blew the lid off the scandal when, on October 25, he issued a report that traced huge sums of money from the city contractors to

Tweed's bank account. Tweed was arrested the next day. On November 2, the chair of the Committee of Seventy, Henry Stebbins, delivered his final report.

"There is not in the history of villainy," he said, "a parallel for the gigantic crime against property conspired by the Tammany Ring. If we fail to punish them, will not the capitalists and merchants of Europe logically conclude that our institutions are a failure, that the strength of American credit is gone and that it is unsafe to lend and sell to a people whose rulers are thieves and whose legislators are robbers and rascals?"

Amazingly, on Election Day two weeks after his arrest, Tweed was re-elected as state senator, amidst allegations of widespread voting fraud. This fact alone is testament to the all-encompassing power and influence of Boss Tweed's reign. Despite their leader's apparent victory, however, Tweed's associates were defeated. In the aftermath of the election, Connolly and Sweeny fled to Canada and Europe. Abe Hall, however, did not give up. He maintained his innocence and refused to resign as mayor. When he was brought to trial in 1872, Hall successfully acted as his own attorney and was acquitted.

After living in London for a few years, Hall finally returned to New York City to live out the rest of his life.

With his cronies defeated or vanished, Tweed became the scapegoat for the corruption that had taken place. He was indicted in December 1871 for fraud and grand larceny. The jury could not reach a verdict, but in November 1873 he was tried again and sentenced to 12 years imprisonment and fined $12,750. The punishment was reduced to one year with a fine of $250 on appeal.

In 1875, almost immediately upon leaving prison, Tweed was arrested on civil charges brought by the state, which sought to recover $6 million in public funds that the Tweed Ring stole. When Tweed could not raise the $300,000 bail, he was sent back to prison to await trial. In prison, he received unusually lenient treatment from his working-class jailers and, at various times, was even allowed leave the premises to visit his home. During such a visit on December 4, he escaped from his guards. He managed to hide himself in New York City for several weeks before he fled to Cuba and on to Spain. While Tweed was working as a deckhand in Spain in 1876, officials

recognized him from his likeness in a
Nast cartoon. He was arrested and
returned to America.

Returned to prison and kept in
strict confinement, Tweed was now a
broken man—much maligned and in
poor health. In 1878, after nearly
two years in prison, William Marcy
Tweed died at the age of 55. He was
buried in Brooklyn.

To this day, no one knows exactly
how much money Boss Tweed and his
cronies stole from the city. Estimates run from
$30 million to $200 million. What is certain is that
Tweed's misdeeds vastly outshine his good deeds in
the historical record. Boss Tweed today is remembered as perhaps the most corrupt politician in
American history.

*By 1878, Tweed
was a broken
man, near death.*

This was not the case in his own day. After
Tweed's death, a journalist from *The Nation* reminded
the public: "Let us remember that [Tweed] fell without
loss of reputation among the bulk of his supporters.
The bulk of poorer voters of this city today revere his
memory, and look on him as the victim of rich men's

malice; as, in short, a friend to the needy who applied public funds . . . to the purposes which they ought to be applied—and that is to the making of work for the working man."

Throughout the nation, however, political reformers rejoiced at the fall of the Tweed Ring. If New York could be saved, they reasoned, so could other cities.

Chapter 6

THE TWEED LEGACY

*T*he motivations and tactics of the men who ran
Tammany Hall until 1871 were undeniably immoral
and criminal. Nevertheless, Boss Tweed did hold the
city of New York together. When the Tweed Ring was
broken, most citizens were relieved to know that
justice was being done. But many also wondered
whether the city could actually be run without the
strong will of a man like Tweed. Major changes were
no doubt called for. But at what price and within what
time frame?

When the corruption of Tweed's government was
finally exposed, the sheer scale of it shocked the
citizenry. Outrage and disbelief sparked a concerted

effort to expose corruption on all levels and to reform government systems so they would no longer be susceptible to such abuses. Soon, the reform movement became the new foundation of New York City politics, and that of many other cities in the nation. The head of the new reformed Tammany Hall was a man named "Honest" John Kelly, who was also a powerful Democratic leader. Kelly had been county sheriff during Tweed's reign but had disagreements with the Boss, which resulted in Kelly taking a prolonged vacation in Europe. A middle-class family man who married the niece of a cardinal, Kelly had a reputation for respectable character that made him a perfect reform-era figure.

The demise of the Tweed Ring occurred at time when the United States was still undergoing a period of enormous change. The entire face of the country continued to evolve as immigrants arrived from nations in every corner of the globe. Some 26 million immigrants arrived in the United States between 1860 and 1900. They came from every continent in the world: 6,060,000 from Northern Europe; 4,576,000 from Central Europe; 1,027,000 from Southern Europe; 928,000 from Canada;

"Honest" John Kelly replaced Tweed as the new head of Tammany Hall.

Between 1860 and 1900, millions of immigrants poured into America from all corners of the world.

688,000 from Eastern Europe; 316,000 from Asia; 9,000 from Australia and New Zealand; 10,000 from Mexico; and 2,000 from Africa.

Ships carrying immigrants from Europe first stopped at Staten Island in New York Harbor. There, passengers underwent a health inspection. Then they would continue to Castle Garden in Manhattan, where all new arrivals were passed through customs. (The well-known stop of Ellis Island did not open until 1892.) From New York City, the immigrants were ready to depart for their new life. Some headed out to the Midwest or Far West on railroads, but 80% remained in New England and the Middle Atlantic states. Millions traveled no farther than lower Manhattan.

America's Workers Unite

Whether immigrants or native-born Americans, the working class grew tremendously with the rise of industry during the Gilded Age. Between 1865 and 1900, the number of people employed in manufacturing in the United States rose from 1.3 million to 4.5 million. Workers' hours were long, the wages low, and working conditions often unsanitary and unsafe.

The concept of a fair wage for an honest day's work did not apply to the average worker. In fact, many working-class families made ends meet only if women and children worked, too. During the late 1800s, approximately 20% of American boys and 10% of girls worked full time in factories and mines.

As corporations and monopolies grew larger, it became clear to many workers that they needed to join forces and demand better wages and working conditions. Some began to form unions. The first national unions were formed by skilled workers: blacksmiths, stonecutters, carpenters. They joined to form the National Labor Union, and actually helped to make 8-hour days a standard for some industries in some states. But the unions lacked the money to influence the political system, and by the early 1870s, the NLU had disbanded.

In 1877, after a depression hit the U.S. economy, almost 20% of the labor force was unemployed. Many industries slashed wages in order to cut costs, and workers responded with riots and strikes. The largest was the Great Railroad Strike of 1877. Railroad employees in Maryland, West Virginia, and Pennsylvania walked off their jobs. When President

Rutherford B. Hayes called out federal troops to break up the strikes, the troops fired into a crowd in Pittsburgh, Pennsylvania, and killed 25 people. In response, mobs set fire to hundreds of trains and buildings. The *New York Times* denounced the Pittsburgh rioters as "hoodlums, rabble, bummers, looters, blackguards, thieves, tramps, ruffians, incendiaries, enemies of society, brigands, rapscallions, riffraff, felons, and idiots."

The violence of the Great Railroad Strike convinced many middle- and upper-class Americans that unions were dangerous, even revolutionary. The fact that many union members were recent immigrants to the United States also made many citizens suspicious of these organizations.

Finally, the labor movement leaders realized that violence could not defeat tycoons or win over public opinion. New leadership was needed. The man who provided that leadership was Samuel Gompers, a cigarmaker, who grew up rolling cigars in his family's tenement apartment in New York City. Gompers was a practical man, not interested in changing the world or the way America did business. He just wanted his workers to have the basics: an 8-hour day, a 5-day

This engraving shows striking railroad workers clashing with troops in Baltimore, Maryland, in 1877.

workweek, and better working conditions. He also demanded the right to negotiate terms and conditions on a regular basis.

When Boss Tweed's influence in New York was at its height in 1870, many immigrants were Irish and German. Thirty years later, Tweed would barely have recognized the Manhattan neighborhoods as he knew them. In addition to the old Irish and German communities, there were Italian, Jewish, and Slavic enclaves. Each group had its own language, customs, religions, newspapers, and shops. Italians joined the Sons of Italy. Lithuanians read the Lithuanian newspaper. Jews went to the Yiddish theater. Similar ethnic neighborhoods and institutions sprang up in cities across the nation—in Boston, Chicago, and San Francisco. Most new immigrants were willing to work for less money than native-born Americans. By 1890, more than half of the labor force in factories was made up of immigrants or the children of immigrants.

In the last decade of the century, as organizations such as Tammany Hall lost respect and power, reformers demanded that city governments take action to help needy residents. A reporter from the *New York Tribune,* Jacob Riis, exposed the slum conditions of the Lower East Side in New York and pushed the government to appoint a tenement house commission. This commission recommended important new construction standards for all new housing. These standards included the addition of fire escapes, running water, and toilets.

Professional fire companies replaced the old independent companies of William Tweed's youth, and trained police became better organized and less corrupt. Safety improved when gas, and later electric, lights were installed along city streets. New water systems brought clean water from reservoirs and mountain streams.

Considering the Gilded Age

Despite the problems of the Gilded Age, the truth is that life became much better for most people in the United States in the nineteenth century. Before industrialization became widespread, practically everything had to be done by hand. Women spun thread by hand; weavers wove cloth by hand; tailors made clothes by hand. Millers ground wheat using only the power of wind or water, and farmers planted fields with only the help of horses or oxen.

"How the Other Half Lives"

In October 1890, a book shocked the middle- and upper-class inhabitants of New York. Written by Danish immigrant Jacob Riis (1849-1914), it was titled *How the Other Half Lives*. For the first time, a published book featured photographs and text together. The book told the heartbreaking story of death and despair in New York's tenements.

Riis, a journalist who worked as a police reporter, often found himself covering stories in the worst of the city's slums. "The sights," he wrote later, "gripped my heart until I must tell of them or burst." He first wrote magazine articles about what he had witnessed. But he felt strongly that the public must see the squalor for itself. The tiny rooms and narrow alleys of the tenements made it too dark for photographs to be taken. In the early 1890s, however, scientists developed a new magnesium powder lamp that flashed a brilliant light when the camera shutter was open.

Jacob Riis

With a group of assistants, Riis made nightly excursions into the foulest streets of the Lower East Side. Finally he had evidence no one could ignore. In the introduction to the book, Jacob Riis wrote:

"Long ago it was said that 'one half of the world does not know how the other half lives.' That was true then. It did not know because it did not care. The half that was on top cared little for the struggles, and less for the fate, of those who were underneath, so long as it was able to hold them there and keep its own seat."

Riis's work influenced a whole generation of reformers and helped direct the role of public housing in the next century.

Everything changed with the development of industry in the United States. For the first time, many people had extra time and extra money—money they could spend on necessities or conveniences, such as ready-made clothes. "Say the worst that can be said about the evils of the [Gilded Age] in America," historian Bruce Catton wrote. "Admit the social irresponsibility of the . . . captains of industry, the brutality with which the factory system ground men down and used them up . . . the fact remains that what was done here meant . . . a more abundant life for all the people."

Increased prosperity and better working conditions also meant increased leisure time. Depending on where one lived, there were church socials, tea dances, or hoedowns. Middle-class women had their gardening, sewing, and reading circles. Traveling shows, such as circuses and Wild West extravaganzas, traveled from cities to small-town America.

In the last decade of the century, people used their increased leisure time to visit music halls or theaters more than ever before. Music was everywhere. Most middle-class homes had a piano, where families gathered for sing-alongs and informal

concerts. Alexander Graham Bell invented the telephone in 1876, and Thomas Edison invented the phonograph in 1877. By 1901, these inventions revolutionized communication and entertainment and were taking their place as fixtures in everyday American life.

A Time for Reform

As the nineteenth century began to wind down, the wonders of the age—mass production, the telegraph, the telephone, and above all the railroad—had made most people more comfortable and better informed than ever before. But communications also made it harder to ignore the many problems that the country still faced. Inequities in opportunity, working conditions, and civil and political rights as well as injustice and dishonesty in government and business were more obvious. Reformers in all fields, from politics to social justice, worked to make the country a better place to live and work.

The fall of Tweed and his Tammany Hall Ring was an important inspiration to many reformers—especially in politics, where the "spoils system" that had controlled jobs in Washington, D.C., came under

Well into the late 1800s, young children worked long hours in factories and used dangerous machines.

fire. When Republican James Garfield became president in 1881, he aimed to do away with the spoils system that led to unqualified and undeserving people filling roles in government. Garfield called for sweeping changes in the civil service. He wanted people to get government jobs based on ability, not political connection. His agenda, however, angered some dangerous people. On July 2, 1881, Garfield was shot and killed by a disappointed office seeker who believed that the spoils system was right. The shock of Garfield's death did a great deal to further spur reform. In 1883, Congress set up the Civil Service Commission to fill jobs in the federal government. Now people could take an exam to prove they were qualified to run the country.

The Muckrakers

At the end of the nineteenth century, a group of committed journalists—following in the reform-minded footsteps of Thomas Nast and George Jones of the *New York Times*—began to alert the public to the ills in American industry. President Theodore Roosevelt called these men and women—who would be known today as investigative journalists—"muckrakers."

Sausage makers at a Chicago meatpacking house, early 1900s. Inset is the Reverend J.R. Day, who defended the meat industry.

"Men with the muckrake are often indis-
pensable to the well-being of society," he
wrote, "but only if they know when to
stop raking the muck."

One well-known muckraker, Lincoln
Steffens, wrote a series of articles that
exposed corruption in city government. Author Upton Sinclair wrote a
novel about Chicago called *The Jungle*
that revealed the filthy practices of slaughterhouses and animal preparation in the city's
meatpacking industry. "There would be meat stored
in great piles in rooms; and the water from leaky
roofs would drip over it," he wrote, "and
thousands of rats would race about on it."

Lincoln Steffens
(above) and Ida
Tarbell (below)
were two of
America's most
prominent
"muckrakers."

Sinclair's exposé prompted the passage
of the Pure Food and Drug Act of
1906. Possibly the most famous
muckraker of all, Ida Tarbell, laid bare
the ruthless business practices of
John D. Rockefeller's Standard Oil.

These writers and others aroused
the public to pressure the government to
pass laws regulating building codes, public

sanitation and public health, food and drugs, honesty in government, and child labor. And finally, public pressure forced Congress to pass laws regulating business monopolies.

New Beginnings

On September 6, 1901, the Gilded Age came to an end. As President William McKinley stood in line to shake hands at the Pan American Exposition at Buffalo, an anarchist named Leon Czolgosz shot him. McKinley died eight days later. The Gilded Age had ended as it had begun—with a presidential assassination.

Bolstered by the intense growth of the Gilded Age, the twentieth century began with the promise of increased prosperity for all Americans. The journey to this point had been a long, arduous one. Workers had been exploited, laws had been flaunted, and many had been free to operate unhindered in order to cultivate their own interests. In many ways, the mid-to-late 1800s had been dark times, made even darker by the corruption of city government and the squalor of city life. Yet, those troubled decades gave rise to a new era of reform and improvement that benefits Americans even to this day. Unfortunately,

little can be said of Boss Tweed and his tenure in Tammany Hall that is positive. The fact remains, however, that Tweed's excesses revealed the vulnerabilities of public servants and political systems and strengthened the resolve to right those terrible wrongs. For that, perhaps, America may actually owe a debt to William Marcy Tweed.

Hester Street, New York City, at the turn of the century, after the Gilded Age had ended

Chronology

The Life of Boss Tweed

April 3, 1823	William Marcy Tweed is born in New York City.
1844	Tweed marries Mary Jane Skaden, daughter of one of his father's business partners.
1850	Tweed is fired from his job as foreman of the Americus Tigers firefighting company.
1850	At the age of 27, Tweed runs for and is elected to public office for the first time.
1852	Tweed is elected to Congress after serving two years as city alderman.
1854	Tweed accepts a post as commissioner of the board of education.
1857	Tweed is elected to the newly formed board of supervisors of the county of New York.
1858	Members of the board of supervisors begin collecting funds to construct a new county courthouse.
1860	Tweed positions himself as kingpin of Tammany Hall.
1863	Even though Tweed is 40 during the draft of 20-45 year old males, he is exempt since he is a city employee.
1863	Tweed is elected Grand Sachem of Tammany Hall. One of his first acts as Grand Sachem is to institute a low-interest loan program whereby men can borrow $300 from Tammany Hall to buy their way out of the draft.
1865	Tweed leads the North's victory parade through New York City after Lee surrenders to Grant at Appomattox Court House.
1870	Tweed is appointed superintendent of public works by mayor and Tweed Ring insider Abraham Hall.

July 29, 1871	James O'Brien, city auditor, exposes the Tweed Ring's corruption in a New York Times article.
September 4, 1871	The Committee of Seventy is appointed to prosecute Tweed.
October 26, 1871	Tweed is arrested.
November 1871	Tweed is re-elected to the Senate.
1873	Tweed is convicted of fraud and grand larceny. He is sentenced to 12 years' imprisonment and fined $12,750; however, the punishment is reduced to one year of prison and a fine of $250.
1875	Tweed is arrested on civil charges brought by the state; he is sent back to prison, unable to raise $300,000 bail. On December 4, Tweed escapes and flees to Spain.
1876	Tweed is recognized from his likeness in a Nast cartoon, arrested, and sent back to prison in America.
1878	William Marcy Tweed dies at the age of 55.

The History of the Nation

1817	Construction on the Erie Canal begins.
1825	Construction on the Erie Canal is completed.
1828	Democrat Andrew Jackson is elected president.
1836	Tammany Hall leader Martin Van Buren is elected president.
April 12, 1861	Fort Sumter, South Carolina, is attacked, signaling the beginning of the Civil War.
July 13-16, 1863	The draft riots, a protest by poor citizens against the draft law, occur in New York City.
April 9, 1865	Confederate general Robert E. Lee surrenders to Ulysses S. Grant at Appomattox Court House, thus ending the Civil War.

April 14, 1865	President Abraham Lincoln is assassinated by John Wilkes Booth.
1868	Ulysses S. Grant is elected president.
May 10, 1869	The Transcontinental Railroad opens, connecting the East Coast with the West Coast.
1870	More than 1,000,000 people, mostly poor immigrants, live in New York City.
1870	Illustrator Thomas Nast publishes many cartoons attacking the Tweed Ring.
1873	Mark Twain publishes *The Gilded Age*. The novel rang so true that the title of his book was applied to the whole era.
1876	Alexander Graham Bell invents the telephone.
1877	Thomas Edison invents the phonograph.
1877	A depression hits the United States economy. Railroad employees in Maryland, West Virginia, and Pennsylvania walk off their jobs, thus beginning the Great Railroad Strike of 1877.
July 2, 1881	President James Garfield is shot by an assassin.
1883	Congress sets up the Civil Service Commission to fill jobs in the federal government.
1890	Two-thirds of New York's population lives in tenements. Jacob Riis shocks the nation with publication of his book *How the Other Half Lives*, which pictorially and textually details the disturbing conditions of life in New York City's tenements.
September 6, 1901	The Gilded Age comes to an end when President William McKinley is assassinated by anarchist Leon Czolgosz.

Glossary

Corrupt Improper or immoral.

Cronies Followers.

Embezzle To steal large amounts of money.

Exploit To take advantage of.

Fraud Act of deceiving or misrepresenting.

Gilded Covered with a thin layer of gold.

Incriminate To show proof of involvement in a crime.

Industrialization Modernization as a result of booming manufacturing businesses.

Infamous Having a reputation of the worst kind.

Influx Coming in.

Infrastructure The framework for a system or organization.

Metropolis A large, important city.

Satire A sarcastic work, often with dissenting political commentary.

Tenement An apartment house that barely meets the minimum standards of sanitation, safety, and comfort, usually located in a city.

Tycoon A businessman of exceptional wealth and power.

Urban Of, relating to, characteristic of, or constituting a city.

Source Notes

Chapter 1

Page 7:   "No Caliph . . ." Quoted in Ric Burns and James Sanders, *New York: An Illustrated History.* New York: Alfred A. Knopf, 1999, p. 160.

Page 8:   "I don't mind what the papers write about me . . ." Quoted in Leo Hershkowitz, *Tweed's New York: Another Look.* New York: Doubleday, 1977, p. 102.

Page 17:   "axes, barrels, and missiles . . ." Quoted in Hershokowitz, *Tweed's New York,* p. 13.

Chapter 2

Page 19:   "an abounding vitality, free and easy manners . . ." Quoted in Burns and Sanders, *New York,* p. 157.

Chapter 3

Page 37:   "called away by an assassin's hand . . ." Quoted in Hershkowitz, *Tweed's New York,* p. 102.

Chapter 4

Page 47:   "I say that you ought to get rich . . ." Quoted in Bernard A. Weisberger, *The Life History of the United States: Steel and Steam.* New York: Time-Life Books, 1964, p. 37.

Page 49:   "Not London, not Paris, not Moscow . . ." Quoted in Burns and Sanders, *New York,* p. 148.

Page 49:   "In a dark cellar . . ." Quoted in Sean Dennis Cushman, *America in the Gilded Age: From the Death of Lincoln to the Rise of Theodore Roosevelt.* New York: New York University Press, 1984, p. 153.

Page 50:   "But to be in it, and not have the distance . . ." Quoted John M. Blum et al., *The National Experience: A History of the United States since 1865,* 4th ed. New York: Harcourt Brace Jovanovich, 1977, p. 447.

Page 51:   "The second year sales would reach 200,000 bottles . . ." Mark Twain, *The Gilded Age.* [Marla Ryan] Garden City, NY: Doubleday, 1965.

Page 52:   "Think what the people of New York are . . ." Quoted in William Riordan, *Plunkitt of Tammany Hall.* New York: E.P. Dutton, 1963, p. 63.

Page 58:   "May God Continue the unity . . ." Quoted in James West Davidson and Michael B. Stoff, *The American Nation.* Englewood Cliffs, NJ: Prentice Hall, 1995, p. 511.

Page 62:	"If you have to pay money..." Quoted in J. Bradford DeLong, *Robber Barons*. http://econ161.berkeley.edu/Econ_Articles/carnegie/delong_moscow_paper2.html.
Page 66:	"I have been insane on the subject of moneymaking all my life. . . ." *New York Daily Tribune*, March 23, 1878.
Page 67:	"The public be damned . . ." Quoted in Joy Hakim, *A History of Us: An Age of Extremes*, 1870-1917. New York: Oxford University Press, 1994, p. 139.
Page 68::	"The millionaires are the bees that make the most honey . . ." Quoted in Hakim, *A History of Us*, p.14.
Page 70:	"The streets are horrible . . ." Quoted in Hakim, *A History of Us*, p. 17.

Chapter 5

Page 71:	"a diamond like a planet . . ." Quoted in Burns and Sanders, *New York*, p. 159.
Page 73:	"The spectacle is appalling . . ." Quoted in Burns and Sanders, *New York*, pp. 159-160.
Page 73:	"I don't think I'll do it . . ." Quoted in David Shirley, *Thomas Nast: Cartoonist and Illustrator*. New York: Franklin Watts, 1998, p. 49.
Page 78:	I fear . . ." Quoted in Seymour J. Mandelbaum, *Boss Tweed's New York*. New York: Ivan R. Dee, Elephant Paperbacks, 1990, p. 81.
Page 79:	"There is not in the history of villainy . . ." Quoted in Mandelbaum, *Boss Tweed's New York*, p. 85.
Page 81-82:	"Let us remember . . ." Quoted in Burns and Sanders, *New York*, p. 162.

Chapter 6

Page 91:	"hoodlums, rabble, bummers, looters, blackguards . . ." Quoted in Cushman, *America in the Gilded Age*, p. 153.
Page 94:	"The sights gripped my heart . . ." Quoted in Burns and Sanders, *New York*, p. 191.
Page 94:	"Long ago it was said that . . ." Jacob Riis. *How the Other Half Lives. [Marla Ryan]* New York, Dover, 1971.
Page 95:	"Say the worst that can be said about the evils . . ." Quoted in Hakim, *A History of Us*, p. 88.
Page 100:	"Men with the muckrake . . ." Quoted in Hakim, *A History of Us*, p. 126.
Page 100:	There would be meat stored . . ." Quoted in Douglas Brinkley, *The American Heritage History of the United States*. New York: Viking, 1998, p. 286.

Further Reading

Aller, Susan Bivin. *Mark Twain.* Minneapolis: Lerner, 2001.

Doherty, Craig and Katherine. *The Erie Canal.* Building America. Woodbridge, CT: Blackbirch Press, 1996.

Gorrell, Gena Kinton. *Catching Fire: The Story of Firefighting.* Plattsburgh, NY: Tundra Books, 1999.

Greenwood, Janette Thomas. *The Gilded Age: A History in Documents.* New York: Oxford University Children's Press, 2000.

January, Brendan. *The Assassination of Abraham Lincoln.* Cornerstones of Freedom. Danbury, CT: Childrens Press, 1999.

Miller, James. *The 1800s.* Headlines in History. San Diego: Greenhaven Press, 2001.

Kallen, Stuart A. *The Civil War and Reconstruction.* Minneapolis: Abdo & Daughters, 2001.

Shuter, Jane. *Henry Ford.* Lives and Times. New York: Heinemann, 2000.

Whitcraft, Melissa. *The Hudson River.* Danbury, CT: Franklin Watts, 1999.

Web Sites

Andrew Carnegie Biography
> www.carnegieclub.co.uk/carnegie_story.html

Boss Tweed Page
> www.pbs.org/wnet/newyork/laic/episode3/topic6/ e3_topic6.html

The Draft Riots of 1863
> www.midtownmedia.com/ndc/Civilwar.html

The Erie Canal
> www.history.rochester.edu/canal

The Gilded Age
> http://ogdensburg.neric.org/~reming/gilintro.html
> www.pbs.org/wgbh/amex/carnegie/gildedage.html

Samuel J. Tilden Biography
> www.spartacus.schoolnet.co.uk/USAtilden.htm

William Marcy Tweed
> www.encyclopedia.com/articles/13160.html

Index

African Americans, 32
Alger, Horatio, 47
Alien and Sedition Acts, 21, 22
American dream, 40

Belmont, August, 76
board of education, 26, 46
bribery, 23, 56, 62, 63, 73, 75
bridges, 6, 54
building codes, 93, 100

Carnegie, Andrew, 10, 64, 65, 66, 67-68, 70
cartoon, 5, 8, 9, 39, 55, 69, 73, 74, 77, 81
Chicago, 44, 57, 60, 67, 92, 98, 100
child labor, 65, 89, 92, 97, 101
cities, 9, 10, 42-45
civil service, 98
Civil War, 27, 29, 31, 34, 35, 68, 77
Committee of Seventy, 76, 79
common people, 22, 24, 48, 52
communication, 72, 97
competition, 64, 65, 67, 68
Connolly, Richard "Slippery Dick", 39, 53-54, 56, 79
corporations, 10, 62, 64-65, 89
corruption, 7, 8, 10, 18, 23, 27, 54, 57, 62, 73, 80, 81, 83, 85, 93, 100, 101
county court house, 7, 27, 75-76
cover-up, 78
Credit Mobilier Scandal, 57
crime, 45, 75

debt, 73, 74-76
Democratic Party, 6, 21, 22, 23, 24, 26, 28, 29, 37, 38, 77, 78
Democratic-Republican General Committee, 7
democratization, 48-50
depression, economic, 89
draft, military, 29-33

economic growth, 9, 10, 38
8-hour work day, 89, 91
election, presidential, 28, 38, 57
embezzlement, 18
Erie Canal, 11, 13, 14-15, 58
Erie Railroad, 61, 63

factories, 9, 38, 40, 56, 89, 92, 97
Federalist Party, 21, 22
firefighting, 17, 18, 71, 93
fires, 17, 45, 91

5-day work week, 91
fortunes, 10, 51, 61, 66
fraud, 75, 79, 80
free speech, 22

Garfield, James, 98
Gilded Age, 8-10, 40-70, 88, 93-97, 101
gold, 63
Gompers, Samuel, 91
Gould, Jay, 61, 63
government, 6, 8, 45, 56, 65, 85, 92, 97, 101
Grant, Ulysses S., 34, 35, 38, 57
Great Railroad Strike of 1877, 89, 91
growth, economic, 9, 10, 38

Hall, Abraham Oakey, 39, 53-54, 56, 79-80
Harpers Weekly, 74, 77
How the Other Half Lives, 94

immigrants, 7, 10, 11, 15, 16, 21, 23, 24-25, 40, 44, 48, 49, 56, 85-88, 91, 92
industrialization, 9, 10, 65, 88, 93, 95
infrastructure, NYC, 24-25, 42, 45
injunction, 78
investors, 10, 61, 62

Jackson, Andrew, 22-23, 57
jobs, 8, 10, 53
Jones, George, 75, 98

Kelly, John, 85
kickback, 68

labor force, 89, 92
labor laws, 65
labor movement, 91
larceny, 80
leisure, 95
Lincoln, Abraham, 29, 30, 35, 37
Lower East Side, 16, 77, 93, 94

McKinley, William, 101
Manhattan, 11, 13, 16, 25, 48, 66, 88, 92
manufacturing, 10, 40, 56, 88
meat packing industry, 98, 100
middle class, 48, 91, 94
military draft, 29-33
millionaires, 68, 69
mines, 38, 89